STUDIO PRESS BOOKS

First published in the UK in 2018 by Studio Press Books,
an imprint of Kings Road Publishing, part of Bonnier Books UK,
The Plaza, 535 King's Road, London, SW10 0SZ

www.studiopressbooks.co.uk
www.bonnierbooks.co.uk

Printed Under License ©2018 Emotional Rescue
www.emotional-rescue.com

7 9 10 8

ISBN 978-1-78741-317-7

Printed in Italy

The Wit & Wisdom of
PROSECCO

STUDIO
PRESS

It was her zest for life and generous disposition that kept her young and happy over the years.
Well, that and Prosecco!

"The top tip in my magazine said that you can keep unfinished Prosecco fizzy, by putting a spoon in the bottle!" she said.
"Ha ha ha!" her friend replied,
"Unfinished Prosecco?!"

Julie had considered exercising,
but didn't...
...for fear of spilling her Prosecco.

s a friend, she wouldn't swap her for the world. For loads of Prosecco possibly, but definitely not the world.

"If I didn't drink Prosecco how would anyone know how much I really, really bloody love them at 2 o'clock in the morning?!"

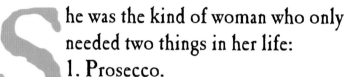

She was the kind of woman who only needed two things in her life:
1. Prosecco.
2. Jamie Dornan.

The beeping noise they'd first thought was coming from her mobile, turned out to be her delivery tanker of Prosecco reversing up the driveway!

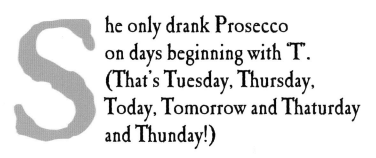

She only drank Prosecco on days beginning with 'T'. (That's Tuesday, Thursday, Today, Tomorrow and Thaturday and Thunday!)

Reading about the terrible effects of drinking Prosecco was enough to make her want to give up reading.

As far as she was concerned, birthdays are nature's way of telling you to drink more Prosecco!

She had one glass of Prosecco for health benefits. (The rest was for witty remarks and amazing dance moves!)

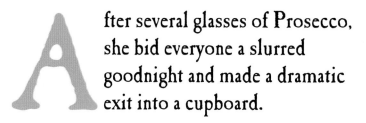fter several glasses of Prosecco, she bid everyone a slurred goodnight and made a dramatic exit into a cupboard.

I'm on the new Prosecco Diet...
So far, I've lost four days!

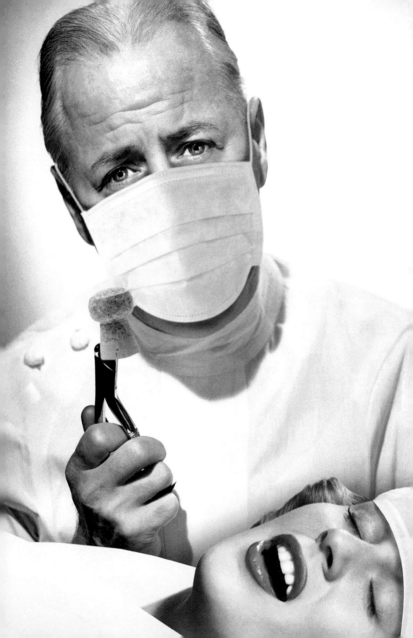

"Blimey! How quickly did she drink the Prosecco on her birthday? I've just found the cork!"

She knew there was a time and a place for Prosecco! In her hand and now!

Sue was suffering from the old 'Women's Problems'...
Not enough Prosecco and chocolate.

Sharon drinks Prosecco because grapes are one of her 5-a-day!

Of course she was bubbly, she was 82% Prosecco!

Gwen didn't need chicken soup for her soul – she preferred Prosecco!

As far as she was concerned, Prosecco was for life, not just for Christmas!

Penelope swore she was never, ever, drinking again! "Ooooh look! Prosecco!"

As it was her birthday, she found a more efficient way of consuming Prosecco.

Whoever said she was 'hard to buy for' must have been as thick as shite!

nna showed absolutely no feelings of guilt when her flatmates asked who had necked that last bottle of Prosecco.